For

_____

on your graduation

From

Rev. Dale Mae

_____

_____

Date

When You Graduate

Signs & signals
for life after
high school

STEVE SWANSON

AUGSBURG Publishing House • Minneapolis

WHEN YOU GRADUATE

Scripture quotations unless otherwise noted are from the Holy Bible: New International Version. Copyright 1978 by the New York International Bible Society. Used by permission of Zondervan Bible Publishers.

Photos: Jean-Claude Lejeune, 10, 28, 44, 54, 118; Michael G. DeVoll, 22, 78; Strix Pix, 66; Dave Anderson, 91; Steve and Mary Skjold, 98.

Library of Congress Cataloging-in-Publication Data

Swanson, Stephen O.
   WHEN YOU GRADUATE.

   1. High school graduates—Prayer-books and devotions—
English.   2. Youth—Prayer-books and devotions—English.
I. Title.
BV4850.S96   1985   242'.63   85-1214
ISBN 0-8066-2157-5

Manufactured in the U.S.A.   APH 10-7086

   3   4   5   6   7   8   9   0   1   2   3   4   5   6   7   8   9

To Ovi, Mooney, Roman,
Foo, Motley, and all
our mid-century classmates.
Thanks for your love and
acceptance—and for all
these memories.

Contents

Prayers

A Note to the Graduate

Someone very special has bought you this book. That someone knows that God has put lots of good stuff inside you, and that same someone hopes that reading this book will help bring more of that good stuff out.

Do read it. Use it. Share it with your family and friends. God bless you mightily at this very special crossroads in your life.

Steve Swanson

The Crush

Marnie had known it was somehow wrong when it first started. In the middle of her senior year she became very aware of Mr. Adams. Before long she was hanging back after his class sneaking glances at him. Sometimes she was the last one to leave. She'd sit at her desk and shuffle her books and pretend she had lots to do.

One day in April he spoke to her. "Well, Marnie, you seem to be getting slower and slower this term. On Tuesday you were the last one out too."

He looked right at her and she felt a shiver go up her back and across both shoulders. "I'm sorry, Mr. Adams. I sometimes get so busy listening and taking notes that I forget to pack up."

"I don't mind," he said. "I never have class next hour anyway."

Marnie remembered what she felt that day—a kind of aching and longing. She had never felt that way about a teacher, but Mr. Adams was so good looking and so smart and so witty when he talked in class. She loved the way he cut down on some of the smart alecs in the back row, like when he stopped Curt Farness cold by saying, "You'll feel better, Curt, when you get over your diaper rash." Curt turned red and didn't fool around for almost a week.

Marnie remembered picking up her books and walking toward the front of the room and trying not to flirt. She did, however, look him in the eye a few split seconds longer than she had ever done with anyone but her own mom. It was a kind of eye-lock. Mr. Adams finally looked away, closing his class record book nervously.

"I have to go now, Mr. Adams. See you tomorrow," she said.

"Bye, Marnie," he replied.

Marnie could remember that day. She could hear his voice saying, "Bye, Marnie," all that afternoon. She remembered going home with his voice ringing in her ears. She had shut her eyes on the bus that day and leaned back, picturing herself on graduation day with his arms around her. She was in her cap and gown and he was saying, "It's OK for us to love each other now that you are out of school."

Marnie had gone on daydreaming and hanging back after class for almost a month. She even had refused a date for the senior prom because of Mr. Adams. For several Sundays she'd sat in the balcony front row at church so she could watch him from behind. Once, in mid-May, when church was over, he had turned and saw her staring at him. He had waved and smiled. He seemed also to have nodded, as if he understood at last what she wanted and had decided that he himself would do something about it.

The next day, with only a bit more than a week before graduation, Marnie decided to change her tactics. She didn't stay as long after class. After their exchange of knowing looks at church, Marnie was going to play hard-to-get. As she passed his desk he said, "Marnie, would you stay a minute, please?"

It worked! she screamed inside herself, feeling that she could probably fly if she just stretched out her arms and pushed off with her toes.

She stood by his desk until everyone had gone. "Sit down," he said, motioning to a front desk. He pulled a desk around to face hers and sat down too.

"Are you in love with me, Marnie?" he asked.

Marnie was struck dumb. She couldn't utter a word. How could she answer such a question?

"I'm going to tell you some things, Marnie, that will help you understand where my heart is. I'm 26 years old, Marnie, and you, you must be, what, 18?"

"Almost," Marnie whispered.

"You probably know I'm not married, but you don't know that I'm engaged. My fiancé's name is Paula. She's a teacher too, but she works in another part of the country. We've been in love for over five years, and we're getting married this summer."

Marnie just swallowed hard. She had nothing to say. Her world was collapsing around her.

"I'm flattered that you like me," Mr. Adams went on. "You're a nice girl, but you should be looking for someone your own age—someone who hasn't got such a head start on you." He smiled.

13

Marnie loved that face. She tried to smile too. It almost worked.

There was silence for a long moment, then Mr. Adams stood up, extended his hand and said, "Friends?"

"Friends," Marnie said, shaking his hand and hurrying out of the room.

"That'll Be the Day"

Andy stood in front of the bathroom mirror modeling his cap and gown. He looked strange in the red robe and the flat hat. He tilted his head from side to side, flipping the tassle back and forth—then, pulling his chin way in, he said in his popular John Wayne imitation, "That'll be the day."

Andy reflected on that phrase. It used to be just a joke sentence, but now he took it as the very motto of his graduation. Tomorrow would indeed be the day— and Andy was excited. He thought back to a Friday afternoon in the spring of his junior year when he had just started to think about graduation and his future.

Andy had had nothing much to do on that Friday, and he didn't have any big plans for the weekend either. He remembered now as he looked in the mirror, that except for going to church and a year more of school and diving on the swim team and playing baseball, he had had nothing particular to do for the rest of his life. That was what had scared him. That was what had led him to walk into the testing and counseling office that Friday a year ago.

"Mr. Graham, I need to talk to someone about my future."

"This isn't a bad place to start," Mr. Graham said. "Come in."

Andy sat down and glanced around the office. There were piles of papers everywhere and four filing cabinets. Mr. Graham probably had a file on everyone in school—and maybe even on kids who had already graduated.

Before he sat down, Mr. Graham pulled open the second drawer of one of the cabinets, flipped through a few tabs, and then lifted out a manila folder. He opened it between them on the desk.

"This is what we know about you," he said, as he outlined the courses Andy had taken, his test scores, grades, and so on. "What's bothering you about your future?" Mr. Graham asked.

"I don't have one. I'll spend one more year here and then I don't know what next," Andy replied.

"Don't you think everyone feels that way?"

"I don't know. Lots of my friends are talking about the future—about going into the service or about college or about jobs."

"There are plenty who are like you, though, who don't know what to do next."

"That doesn't make it any easier."

"I know. What would you like to do?"

"I'd like to go to college, I guess, but my grades aren't good enough."

When Andy mentioned grades, Mr. Graham flipped back a few sheets in the folder and turned up the transcript again. "Let's see," he said. "Well, you certainly haven't been an honor student, but you've done well in some things. You could get into a lot of colleges, even if your next year's grades stayed about the same."

"What colleges?"

"We have a book here that lists them all. These figures here," he pointed, "are statistics on each one that more or less shows us how tough they are to get into and to stay in. Like here. Here's one you probably couldn't get into—and here's one you could. See the difference in numbers?"

Andy nodded. There was a silence. Then Mr. Graham asked, "What do you want to do with your life?"

"What I really want to be is a preacher."

"That means quite a bit of school."

"I know. That's what scares me."

"What church do you go to?"

"Messiah, over on Second Street."

"Pastor McLennon's church?"

"Yes."

"Why don't you tell him about your dream, and ask him about the training?"

"I will. I'll stop in today."

Andy's mind flashed forward into the present. As he stood in cap and gown, he was thankful that he had good friends like Mr. Graham and Pastor McLennon who had taken time to help him. He had found motivation, he had found a handle on the future, and he had found a reason to get better grades. He had spent his senior year preparing for some fairly demanding tomorrows.

Andy would graduate the next day. He and his parents would be pleased to see his name on the B honor roll as well. If someone had told him a year earlier that he would be an honor student, he would have laughed, spread his feet way out wide, pulled in his chin, and drawled, "That'll be the day."

The Best Year of Her Life

Lori tried to remember how many older people had said to her in the last few years, "Enjoy your senior year. It will be the best year of your life."

She was in her senior year. In fact, she was almost through her senior year—and it had been one of the *worst* years of her life. To begin with, she and Marlene, her best friend, had had a stupid fight the summer before, and they only now were beginning to do things together again. That was eight months without a best friend. Best year of her life? No way.

It seemed, too, that so many of her classmates had gotten so serious. They were all talking college or electronics school or computer school or jobs. They just weren't the fun kids they had been the last few years.

One of the casualties of all this seriousness was school spirit, or at least it seemed so to Lori. Take homecoming, for instance. Lori was on the senior class float committee and must have called 15 kids, the kids you could have counted on as sophomores and juniors. Only three showed up. The float was a joke. In fact the whole homecoming was a joke. Nobody yelled at the game. And the dance. Lori was only one of many senior girls who went to the dance without dates—or didn't even go—because there weren't any older boys to ask them out any more. Best year of her life. Ha.

Things were about the same at home, though. No, they weren't. They were better. Her younger brothers were getting more fun to be around. They weren't the pests they used to be. And her parents were getting more understanding. They were all beginning to act more like a family. In fact during Easter break the whole family went bowling and had a really good time.

The more Lori thought about her senior year in school, the more she realized that West High School was only a small part of her life. Maybe that's what was bothering her. Maybe as they all got ready to leave old West High they were being forced to see high school as only a small fragment of a whole life.

Lori began to look at the other factors in her life, the other influences and segments. There was her home, her family, her church—and that included her faith. There were her alone times too. She wasn't thinking of the lonely times but the *alone* times—the good times alone. She remembered mornings when she woke up early and thought or prayed. She remembered evenings when everyone else was gone and she baked brownies or just curled up in dad's leather chair and read for two hours. Those were parts of her life that were super good every year, not just in her senior year.

What if, she thought, what if her senior year really *were* the best year of her life? That wouldn't leave much to look forward to, would it? That would be awful. Surely some year in college would be a better year. Maybe the first year of her marriage would be great. She hoped so. She hoped he, whoever he was, wherever he was, would love her and make her feel special and make her years just great. Maybe she would have children. They would raise them together. Those would be good years too.

Lori shook her head and came back to the here and now. She was standing in front of her open locker daydreaming, the last bell buzzing in her ear. She grabbed her books, slammed the locker door shut, and ran for class.

This may not be the best year of my life, she said to herself, *but I'm going to be sure it's not the worst. I'm going to enjoy the rest of it, no matter what anyone else does.*

Cut from the Team

Howie was still angry about the basketball team. He counted the months on his fingers: November, December, January, February, March, April. Six months. Half a year. Two-thirds of a school year. And every time he thought about it, he seethed inside.

Coach Beech had cut him from the team—and in his senior year, too. If he really *was* no good at basketball, they should have cut him in his sophomore year. Then he could at least have gone out for wrestling or something. As it was he had to spend the winter of his senior year doing nothing.

Doing nothing was the problem. Howie was so angry that he had let *everything* go—his schoolwork, his chores at home, his friends on the basketball team. About the only thing he didn't give up was the youth group at church.

One day, Mr. Wood, Howie's math teacher, asked him to stay after class. "Howie," he said after the other students had gone, "you've gotten into a terrible slump, and there's only a month of school left."

"I know," Howie said, looking at his feet. Of all his teachers, Mr. Wood was his favorite. They even went to the same church.

"I went and looked at your transcript this morning. You are in some danger of not graduating."

"I guess I'd just quit then. I wouldn't come back here," Howie blurted out.

"Is it so bad?"

"This year it was."

"What was so bad about this year?"

"I don't want to say."

They talked for five more minutes and Howie said nothing about the basketball team. Nice as Mr. Wood was, he was still a *school* person.

"You and Pastor Michaels are friends, aren't you?"

"I guess so," Howie said. Pastor Michaels was the main reason Howie had stayed with the youth group. Even in November when he had to take the ribbing about being cut he still came. Their youth pastor was someone special.

"I'd like to call him and tell him about your school work."

"I don't know what good that would do. My mother has been here twice."

"I don't know either, but it's worth a try. Will you try?"

"I guess." Deep down, Howie wanted to tell someone.

Mr. Wood arranged a meeting that very afternoon. Howie went to the church after school and he and pastor Michaels talked—and talked and talked. Howie found out that Pastor Michaels had played hockey in *his* senior year—but on the J.V. squad.

"That's almost worse than being cut," Pastor Michaels said. "You get out there and play with the kids, the freshmen and sophomores. Then you dress and sit in the stands to watch your classmates play the *real* game."

They talked more and arranged to get back to Mr. Wood for help in setting up some crash tutoring. They talked about college. Pastor Michaels made college sound fun, worth trying.

The climax came when Howie was almost out the door. Pastor Michaels said, "Do you know, Howie, that I played college hockey?"

"You did? And after playing J.V. in high school?"

"Sure. I won two letters. People develop at different times. I hit my stride in college. Besides," he said, putting an arm around Howie's shoulders, "you can't let just one coach shut you down."

"I suppose not," Howie said, thinking that if he hurried, he could maybe get back to school in time to get some of his books.

I'm Losing All My Friends

"What scares me most," Lisa told Mr. Archer, "is losing all my friends."

"You don't really lose them," he said.

"But I do. Nobody else from here is going to the same college I am, and I don't know anyone there. I'll be all alone my whole freshman year."

"How many freshmen are they expecting there next fall?"

"About 500."

"I'll bet you'll be the only one who doesn't bring a few friends along."

Lisa smiled and swallowed hard. Mr. Archer was known for his sharp wit and biting satire. "Another of Mr. Archer's arrows in the heart," the kids would say after someone had been cut down in his sociology class. Lisa liked him, though. Most of the kids did. And he was right. There would be dozens, probably hundreds of kids at college who would be alone.

Lisa thought about what Mr. Archer said as she walked home that day. In less than four months she would be on a beautiful campus, all alone for the first time. She had gone away before, but never like that.

Lisa remembered her German class, and how they had done a million projects to earn money and had all gone to Germany for three weeks—but she had gone with friends and classmates. She remembered also the weeks she had spent at church camp and 4H—but they were also weeks spent with old friends.

But as she thought of the camps, especially church camp, Lisa thought of the two or three really good friends from nearby towns that she had met at camp. They wrote, they exchanged Christmas cards, they kept in touch. Might not college be like that? Might she not, wouldn't she *certainly*, meet new friends in the first week, maybe even the first day?

And she would have a roommate. That was something to think about. Maybe her roommate would become a friend. Maybe even a best friend. That was something to think about. That was something to pray about.

And her old friends? They would still be friends, wouldn't they? Mr. Archer was right about that. She would see some of them when she came home for weekends or holidays. Any of them, all of them, were as close as the phone or the mailbox.

Redefining the Future

When Todd thought about his future, he realized how often he had redefined his goals. He couldn't remember being an infant, of course, but he could imagine his future then as being connected with being warm and fed and hugged and kept in clean diapers.

He could remember grade school, though, and how the future then was measured in class outings and in which friends he was going to play with, and whose birthday party he was going to be invited to.

In junior high it was sports and vacations and for the first time, girls. Todd had first noticed Jan in eighth grade. She had never really noticed him, though, and the harder he tried to make her notice, the less she seemed to care.

That lasted two years. Then suddenly Jan was swallowed up in other friendships and other concerns. For the last two years Todd had been jockeying for positions on teams and places in peer groups and trying to do well in his classes. It was a nerve-wracking business but he had managed to be both reasonably popular and also a good student.

But now, as a senior, his future seemed more serious, more threatening. Looking backwards, the birthday parties, his crush on Jan, his friends and teams and groups—and even his class work—didn't seem to have amounted to much. Oh, he knew they had all contributed to making him who he was. He didn't have to be much of a psychologist to realize that. But now he was looking to a tougher future—college, a job, supporting himself. That seemed a whole lot more frightening.

Todd wished someone would tell him what to do. He had applied at four colleges. His grades were good. Maybe all four would accept him. Then what? How would he decide? Would God show him a vision from heaven? How did people decide such things? He couldn't figure that out.

He asked his dad that night. "How did you decide which college to go to?"

"I didn't really have to decide," his dad said. "The college was right in my hometown and your grandpa worked there as a carpenter. If I went to school there, I didn't have to pay any tuition at all—and I could live at home too. Your Aunt Sue and I both went there. We couldn't have afforded to do anything else."

"But it's not that way with me. I may have four choices. How will I decide?"

"It may be partly money with you too. You will get some financial aid. You may decide to go to the school that costs the least."

"I suppose so."

"But there are other factors. How far away it is, for example, travel expenses and all. And two of them are church schools. That's a big factor. The percentage of Christian teachers and students is higher there. I guess your mom and I would encourage you to consider that factor strongly."

"I wish I had a crystal ball."

"No one has. All big decisions are hard. But you will make it. And one sign of maturity is that after you make a decision, you do your best to make it work."

"I'll try, dad, I really will."

"I know you will. When we have your acceptances in hand we'll study them and we'll write some letters and we'll make some phone calls and we'll pray. It will work out. Don't worry."

Can Romance Survive Graduation?

"I'm really scared," Sue said.

"About what?" Paul asked.

"About us. About your going off to the U."

"I'll be home weekends."

"I know that, but it's all those girls."

"Oh, come on."

"I've seen them. I was there for our band workshop last fall. Every other girl looked like Hollywood."

"The Hollywood types don't interest me."

"You'd rather have them ugly, like me, right?" She was smiling as she said it.

"I like them nice like you."

"But what if you meet someone you like better?"

"I suppose that could happen. I'm not going out looking, though."

"I'll bet you will."

"I won't be a hermit—but I won't be hunting either. I'm satisfied with you."

"I want you to be more than satisfied. I want you to be convinced."

The following Sunday, Sue and Paul sat together in church. As they were going out, Pastor Sherwin stopped them. "Are you ready for the university, Paul?" he asked.

"I guess so. I hope so."

"And what are your plans, Sue?" he asked.

"I'm going to work this year, then decide about school after that."

"Are you staying here in town?"

"Yes. I have a job at Lundeen's Accounting."

"So you're going to try to keep your romance going at long distance?" the pastor asked.

"We're going to try," Paul said. "We were talking about that this week."

"We're wondering," Sue broke in, "if we'll meet and date other people while we're apart."

"What do you think, pastor?" Paul asked.

"I think you should. I always think you should, until you are absolutely sure of each other—until you are engaged or almost engaged. You aren't engaged, are you?"

"No." Sue and Paul said it together. They all three laughed.

"Well at least you agree on that," the pastor said. "You are only 18 or so now. You have some time to decide. I spend at least a quarter of my time counseling troubled couples. They are fighting, they are separated, they are divorced. In many cases they married too young, before they became what they were going to be."

"What do you mean by that?" Paul asked.

"The years from 18 to 25," the pastor went on, "are very formative. You take a boy who is all athlete in high school, who goes off to college and gets interested in music or art or anthropology. That cheerleader he thought was so special in high school might not be right for him then."

"Unless she changes too," Sue said.

"That's what makes some childhood sweetheart marriages work. Either they were very wise when they were very young, or God simply gave them to each other in a special way, or else they were pre-programmed to change in the same directions. More often than not, though, they end up in my office or with some other counselor, or in the divorce courts. You don't want that, do you?"

"No." Again they both said it together and once again they all laughed.

"I think you should date other people this year. We could get together next Christmas and talk about what happened."

"I think I'd like that," Sue said.

"Me too," said Paul.

Ending the War

John's flash of insight came just before Easter. He was in his senior history class studying World War II and the mid-century troubles between the nations of the world. He studied about what the various nations had wanted or hoped to get out of a war. Then it came to him: *I have been at war with my parents for two years,* he thought. *Except that it's been a "cold war."*

Somehow things had gotten twisted many months earlier, and John's parents had become the enemy. Like in a war, they were the ones trying to limit his movements and his territory and his possessions and his friendships.

John wondered what could be done. Next year he would go to Manning Institute to study electronics. That probably meant leaving home for at least a year, maybe two. He didn't want to go away still at war.

He knew, though, that he couldn't just walk into the kitchen some morning waving a white flag and asking for peace. He didn't want to surrender anyway. He just wanted them to recognize him as a person, to know that he could make decisions too, even if some of them were the wrong decisions.

He asked his friend Steve after school, "Do you fight with your parents?"

"I guess so. Sure I do."

"What about?"

"Oh," said Steve, "about how late I stay out, who I run around with, what I do with my spare time—stuff like that."

"It's the same with me. It's like we were in a war."

"That's what my dad calls it—*a war of wills*—what they want against what I want."

"How do we get out of it?" John asked.

"I don't think we ever do, really, but it gets better. My parents don't bother my older brother much at all."

"I don't have an older brother."

"You *are* the older brother."

"I guess I am. But how can I get them off my back? How can I make peace?"

"One way is to do more of what they want—like cleaning your room, for instance. I cut the battles with my mother in half by setting my alarm 10 minutes earlier and cleaning my room before school. Now she doesn't holler at me for a messy room *or* for not getting up."

"That would be hard for me."

"It was hard for me at first. You only have two months of school left. Why not try it?"

"Maybe I will. Maybe that will be my white flag. Maybe if I surrender just a little bit, maybe something good will come of it."

John thought of how Germany and Japan had been the Allies' enemies and how surrender had been a good thing for them—and for us. Enemies can become friends. He waved good-bye to Steve and headed for home.

Surrender, he thought, *was a big idea in last week's Sunday school lesson, the prodigal son. When we surrender to God, when we are ready to come home and become his servants, then suddenly we are friends, suddenly we recognize his love.*

John knew that cleaning his room was not a total surrender, but it was a place to start. He had two months to surrender to his parents, to sue for peace. It would be worth a try. He would ask God for help and he would try.

All Dressed Up and No Place to Go

"If one more person asks me what I'm going to do next year, I'm going to scream." Missy slammed her books down on Martha's kitchen table. "Why couldn't I be like you with big plans and goals?"

"I only know what I *want* to do. I haven't done it yet. I haven't even started."

"But you know *where* to start," Missy said, taking the glass of cola Martha handed her. "I don't even know *that*, and everyone's asking. Over half our class is going to college. I'm not. Some of the rest are going to trade schools. I'm not. Or into the service. I'm not. Or have jobs waiting for them. I don't. I feel like some special brand of freak not knowing anything, not having *any* plans."

"Why don't you take a test—like a vocational test?"

"I did take one of those. Do you know what it said? It said I should be in food preparation."

"You mean like a cook?"

"Sure. Can you see me in the kitchen at the Fireside Cafe for the rest of my life?"

"It's honest work."

"I know that, but cooking is my hobby, not my calling. I don't want to spend my life cooking."

"Knowing how to cook is a good thing for a *wife* to know how to do," Martha said, smiling.

"I said I don't want to spend my life cooking. That means for a husband *or* for a hash factory."

"Well, you know one thing you *don't* want to do. How about something you *do* want to do?"

"Sleeping is my favorite thing."

"No one gets paid for that."

"I know. Maybe I could demonstrate beds or couches."

"Sounds pretty specialized."

Then, as if some strange switch had been turned inside her, instead of laughing, Missy was crying. "Come on, Missy, it's not that bad," Martha said, wrapping her arms around the crying girl.

"But it is," Missy sputtered between sobs. "The world is so big and so scary and I don't have a place in it."

"But you will. God knows you're here. He has plans for you."

"Well why doesn't he tell me about them?"

"Maybe it's still a secret. Maybe you're going to be a great actress or a TV anchorwoman or a deep sea diver with Jacques Cousteau."

Missy couldn't help laughing.

"That's better," Martha said.

"But I still don't know what to do."

"Let's talk to someone who knows something about it. My dad meets lots of people in his work. Maybe he'd have an idea. And how about Pastor John or Karen in the youth office? They might have some ideas."

"Maybe so."

"Let's go over to church right now and see if anyone's there. Then you stay for supper and we'll talk to my dad. We'll find some place for you to start your life. We'll get you going."

"I hope so."

"We will." Martha grabbed Missy's wrist and they flew out of the kitchen and down Martha's back steps.

Job Hunting

I never thought it would be this hard.

Dale had been looking for a job for over a month. He had started the first week in February and now it was the middle of March. Dale wanted to work after he graduated in May. He had decided to take any decent job he could find. His only rule was that he wanted to do it himself. His father had some connections through his union and his mother knew people at church. They both had offered to help him look, to get him an interview at least. "I'm going to do it on my own," he had said to both of them.

Dale was indeed trying to do it on his own. He had gotten passes from the office every afternoon for a month. For the last two hours each day, instead of study hall, he was checking out the places he had listed the night before. He hunted through the newspapers and scoured the yellow pages each night, then the next day he would make two or three stops, asking about openings, trying to get an interview, working at getting a job.

Dale was getting discouraged. On March 15th he sat down with his job hunting notebook and counted the contacts he had made. There were over 40. He had tried for 40 jobs; he had had only five interviews; he had gotten no job.

Dale's father walked in as he was sitting there looking sour. "Nothing yet?" his father asked.

"Nothing. I just counted. I've made 40 contacts and had only five interviews."

"Maybe you're not going at it right."

"Don't tell me another time that I can get a job at your warehouse. I know that. I'm trying to do it on my own."

"You don't have to work at my warehouse. Just let me make some contacts for you. You've given it a fair shot. No one would fault you for that."

"I don't know."

"And your mother has contacts too. Let us help you."

"I'll think about it."

Dale did think about it. He thought about it all weekend—and prayed about it too. He searched his mind for Bible stories in which people were helped in getting what they wanted. He knew that Jesus had helpers—the disciples, and so had John the Baptist. Paul had Barnabas and Timothy. He remembered Moses, whose brother Aaron was such a big help to him. These were not stories of job hunting, though; these were stories of great heroes of faith. His was a much simpler concern.

As Dale sat musing upon his dilemma, he thought of the story of Ruth. *Seems like she got some help at first,* he thought. Dale reached for his Bible on the shelf by his bed. He found the book of Ruth and started reading it. As he read the story, he began to feel sorry for Naomi and all her troubles. He was touched by Ruth's words to her mother-in-law. He remembered hearing those words sung at his cousin's wedding.

As he continued the story he saw how Boaz helped Ruth because he loved her. He was also reminded that Naomi had been in Moab, a foreign country, but now she was in Judah, in Bethlehem, the birthplace of Jesus.

Naomi and Ruth got help when they came home, just like the prodigal son did. Help sometimes comes from home. *Who else is more apt to help us?* Dale thought. *Who wants to help more than those who love us, those at home?*

Dale closed his Bible, put it back on the shelf, and walked downstairs. His father was reading the Sunday paper. "Dad," Dale said. His father looked up from the paper. "I've thought about what you said, about helping me find a job."

"Yes."

"I've decided I'd like you to try."

"I'll try. We'll try. We'll do more than try. We'll have something for you soon."

"Just like Boaz."

"What?" his father said. But Dale was already off looking for his mother.

Starting All Over Again

The idea of being a senior really pleased Ginny. "We're the big shots now," she said to herself. She said the same thing to her friend Bill the first week in the fall. "Isn't it great to be seniors at last?"

"I guess so. I don't feel much different, though."

"We aren't any different. The only thing is that we're the oldest ones now, except for the teachers."

"That does make a difference. I've thought of that in football practice. Last year if someone would fake me out or get a good block on me, either in practice or in a game, I'd be apt to say, 'Well, after all, he's older.' "

"That's what I mean. We're the oldest. If I don't make first chair clarinet this year it's because someone is better, not older."

"We don't have to take any guff from anyone either. Remember Senior-Sophomore Week two years ago?"

"Do I!" exclaimed Ginny. "I was assigned as slave to Marlene Johnson. She made me follow her around and carry her books all week. I had to wear red lipstick spots on my cheeks and on my nose too. I looked like Bozo the Clown."

"It was kind of fun. Embarrassing but fun. This year it's our turn."

"Right. We're the seniors now. We're the big shots."

As Ginny walked away she reflected on the stages in her life. She had gone to nursery school for two years. The second year was like a senior year. She knew how everything was done, where everything was kept, and she was the teacher's main helper most of the year. Then it was kindergarten and she was just as lost as anyone else. That went on until sixth grade when they were the oldest again. Then in junior high she started over, then in senior high.

Life is one long series of starting over, Ginny thought. *I may be a big shot now, but next year it's back to being a freshman.*

Ginny thought of all the starting over times that people had to face in an entire life: You finish college and you are immediately an entry-level freshman in a new job. You get married and you begin a whole new stage in life. And she thought about Mrs. Williams, whose husband died and she remarried. That was really starting over. Retirement too is a starting over.

Ginny thought about death and all she had heard in church and read in the Bible about death and life after death. *Now that's really starting over. There aren't any big shots in heaven,* Ginny thought, *Jesus said so himself.*

Ginny began to think that maybe all this starting over again and again through life was a preparation for death. *Maybe God doesn't want us to feel like big shots for too long,* she thought. *Maybe that is against his way.*

Ginny then thought of Jesus. He was the biggest big shot of all—the Son of God and everything. But he never acted like it. He never but one day in his whole life acted like a king. And even on that day he rode on a donkey.

Ginny decided then and there that even if she was a senior, she wouldn't act like a big shot. Not even during Senior-Sophomore Week.

Doubting Thomas

"They should have named me Thomas," Paul said to himself as he walked out of church on the Sunday after Easter. Listening to the sermon about Thomas reinforced everything that had been troubling him lately. Maybe part of the problem was that he had been up so extra early the previous Sunday helping with the youth breakfast. He had fried bacon for two hours, served tables for an hour, and then gone to church. A week later he still hadn't recovered. Maybe it was just being tired all week that did it, that brought all these doubts to a head.

Paul walked along the dusty sidewalk toward home, musing on his doubts. It wasn't just today. For many weeks now the amazing stories and scenes from the New Testament were going through his mind. It had started with the miracles.

Just before Christmas one of his teachers had told a joke about a hunting dog that walked on water. The punch line was the fellow hunter's observation, "I see your dog can't swim." Paul had laughed at the joke like all the others in class, but it reminded him that walking on water was a Jesus story. Paul had no problems with Jesus walking on water, but then he thought about Peter. Peter had done it too. But Peter was just an ordinary person. That took some faith to swallow—Peter walking on water—even though he did sink later.

Then it was the feeding of the 5000 and the healings and the stilling of the storm. Paul's mind was being bombarded by these stories and the faith that it took to believe them. At his worst times, he wondered if he believed any of it. Usually this was late at night when he tossed and squirmed under the covers, trying to get to sleep.

Even at the best of times, though, he couldn't get back to that simple, comfortable faith of just a couple of years before. On his confirmation day, for instance, he had believed it all. He had looked up to the picture of Jesus on the altar and had believed every word, every story, every miracle.

He knew that Thomas had lived through his doubts. The pastor had said so in his sermon—and the Bible was clear on that. But Thomas *knew* Jesus. He had *seen* the miracles and he could see the wounded hands and feet and side. Paul thought of Jesus with the child on his knee. He knew the faith of a child was the ideal. How could he recover that? Where had it gone?

Paul mused upon his doubts for two more weeks. Then one evening he asked his dad. "Do you ever have doubts, dad?"

"Doubts about what?"

"About religion and the Bible and all that."

49

"Sure I do."

"Isn't that bad?"

"I guess it is, in some ways. But doubts can also be good."

"How?"

"I think they make us grow. If we didn't have doubts, we wouldn't ever have an adult faith. We'd live in Santa Claus land forever."

"But Jesus said that childhood faith is good."

"That's right. But I don't think Jesus wants us to have a child*ish* faith. He wants us to have a child*like* trust in God's love—and also to use our minds to think and ask questions."

"Do you think Jesus likes it when we ask questions?"

"Sure. He doesn't want to keep us from growing up. He knows what the real world is like. He knows about thieves and hypocrites and crooked tax collectors and prostitutes. He knows that a childish faith can't handle all that."

"So it's OK to doubt like Thomas did?"

"Yes. And like your Grandma Bauer did."

"I can't imagine her ever having had doubts."

"This Sunday when we're over there, you ask her about some of the old times. Ask her about when the prairie fire burned them out, and when your great Uncle Ernie was killed by a horse."

"I didn't know about an Uncle Ernie."

"He was your Grandfather Bauer's brother."

"She's really been through some stuff."

"Yes she has. That's why her faith is so special."

50

Things Left Undone

Arlene was pulled up short when she read Romans 7:19, "For what I do not do is not the good I want to do; no, the evil I do not want to do—this I keep on doing." There was only one week of school left. Arlene was graduating. She should have been bubbling with excitement. Instead she was riddled with regrets.

Arlene certainly didn't have St. Paul's cosmic sense of good and evil. She wasn't doing anything so terribly wrong. But she was aware of many things she *hadn't* done. There were resolutions she had only pretended to keep. There were hopes that had been sidetracked, dreams that had never materialized. There were friendships she hadn't made, helping hands she hadn't offered. Arlene wished she had done better.

She finished her devotions with a prayer and reached for a scratch tablet she kept on her desk. *I'm going to list all the things I should have done in the last few years,* she thought, then shuddered at how long a list that was bound to be. She poised her pencil above the page, then bending deeply over her desk, she began to write:

> —*visit Mrs. Sheffelbein*
> —*be better friends to Mary and Tina*
> —*try to understand mom*

Arlene lifted her pencil and began staring out the open window. She wondered why she so often had been sidetracked in her good intentions, why she was sitting here frowning with regrets.

She thought about that for a while and couldn't figure it out, exactly, until she started remembering specific instances. One time she had intended to visit Mrs. Sheffelbein, and Tina had called to go shopping. Another time she had gotten almost ready to go and then remembered she hadn't sorted her clothes for the choir trip. The problem was selfishness.

Mrs. Sheffelbein never knew she had come out second best those times. There was no schedule. There were no promises. But Mrs. S. had been such a good friend to Grandma Frame before she died. It wasn't fair now, for her to live all alone and have hardly anybody visit her, especially young people like herself. Arlene had regrets all right.

What do I do about regrets? Arlene asked herself. *What does a Christian do about regrets?* She decided that forgiveness was a place to start. She first bowed in prayer and asked God's forgiveness. Then she went to the phone book and looked up Mrs. Sheffelbein's number, writing the numbers boldly after her name on the "regret list." Arlene would ask her forgiveness too—

and then set a time, a specific, hard-and-fast time to pay a call.

Before dialing, Arlene took another look at her list. Instead of thinking there was *only* one week left, she could be more positive. There was not only a week of school but also a whole summer. She would try to visit Mrs. S. that very day, and that week in school she would re-cement her friendships with Mary and Tina—and she would open new negotiations with her mom. "I can do all things through Christ," Arlene whispered to herself, and aimed a much more confident finger at the numbers on the kitchen telephone.

A Girl My Age

Mark paused on the steps of the college library to watch some of the other freshmen pour through the big, oak doors. He was watching for Amy. He had met her the first day of orientation week. There had been some nice looking girls in his high school, but this was something else. There were about 400 in his freshman class, half of them girls. Amy wasn't the only attractive one.

Mark wondered if he had a chance with Amy or if it would be the same here as in his high school. He remembered the crush he had had on Dawn Carter in ninth grade. He had watched her for over a month, trying to get up courage to talk to her. He never saw her after school—it was as if she disappeared—so he watched for her in the hallways, and he knew just where to look, just where she usually sat at assemblies. He nearly failed first-year typing because Dawn was in his class and sat at a desk directly on his left, two rows away. Every time he sneaked a look at her, he would hit a wrong key or jam six letters together into the throat of his machine like a miniature steel wigwam frame.

Mark's big chance had come at the class Halloween party. He and Dawn were kneeling at the same washtub, bobbing for apples. Someone down the line was horsing around and both Mark and Dawn were knocked off their knees and onto the gym floor. They picked themselves up and talked and laughed for several minutes as they were wiping themselves off with towels. Mark cranked up his courage to full power and said, "If you aren't doing anything, I'd like to walk you home."

"I *am* doing something afterwards, Mark. Rick Allen is picking me up."

"Oh," Mark said.

"Sorry," she said, turning to go. "Thanks for asking though."

That's the way it always was in high school. The girls you wanted to be with went with the older boys. Rick Allen was a senior, played hockey, was on the student council—and had a car. Mark had no chance against him. No chance at all.

But three years later when he himself was a senior, he could have asked Dawn out. She would have gone, too. He was by then a regionally ranked tennis player and soloed with the choir. But by then he wasn't interested in Dawn. By then he wasn't interested in any of the girls in his high school. Somehow he was too busy—and in a subtle way that even he wouldn't have been able to explain, he was saving dating and girls for college.

Mark pulled himself out of his memories as he pulled the library door open. *Amy must be in there already.* Almost everyone had gone in. He had to hurry. *I hope it will be better here,* he thought. *I hope it doesn't matter what class you're in or how old you are.* He knew better, though. He had seen the football players, on campus early, watching the freshmen girls in the cafeteria, Amy included.

Maybe I'm putting too much sweat into this business, he thought. *Maybe this is a place where those who don't get picked off by seniors right away, maybe they're the best ones. And maybe there are girls around who just want to be friends. Maybe here we won't all have to pair off so much. Maybe making friends first is the way to find that one special friend anyway!*

Even though he was already two minutes late, Mark leaned his head against the door frame of the lecture hall. "Lord," he prayed silently, "Help me to make lots of friends here, boys and girls both. And help me to recognize that special one when she comes along."

Mark pulled open the door and walked into the lecture hall. There was an empty seat next to Amy. *What luck,* he thought.

Off to the City

"So. You're going off to the big city next year," Grandma Lamb said to Kim as they worked together washing the graduation reception dishes.

"Yes, I am, Gram," Kim replied.

"I don't know how you children have the courage. Sakes alive! I'd be frightened out of my wits. When I was your age, we were scarcely allowed out after dark."

"Oh, Gram."

"It's true. When I was your age, if I had told my father I wanted to live in the city, in an apartment—and alone—"

"I won't be alone," Kim interrupted. "There are two other girls."

"Nonetheless, if I had even suggested such a thing to your great grandfather, he would have called in Doc Zander to have my head examined or given me a sedative."

"What year was it, Gram, when you were my age?"

"I graduated in the class of 1930. The year after the Crash."

"What was your graduation like?"

"It was very austere. There was no money at all. Not many of us had new dresses. Graduation gifts were inexpensive, mostly hand-made. I'll bet my whole graduating class put together didn't get gifts equal to what you alone have gotten the last few days."

Kim's grandma went on describing her youth for 20 minutes or more, until at last they were washing off the counters and hanging up the wet dish towels to dry. Kim hugged her grandma, thanked her, then went upstairs to dress for her date with Del.

She sat on her bed and stared at the maroon cap and gown hanging on the closet door. *Times really have changed,* she thought. *Grandma's life sounded so simple—finish school, teach in a country school a couple of years, marry a farmer, raise kids, work. So simple.*

Kim had no such handle on the future. All she knew was that it wouldn't be simple. She liked Del but knew she would never marry him. She had no idea what her life in the city would be like beyond her courses at the computer center. Would she have any social life at all? Would there be temptations too harsh for her to face? Was it really the wicked city?

As Kim sat there musing, part of the Lord's Prayer popped into her mind: "Lead us not into temptation," and that led to: "nor does [God] tempt anyone." She said it out loud, remembering James 1:13 from Sunday school.

God has plans for my good, she thought. *I will be the same person there that I am here. I will look after myself, trust in God, and live by the same standards I always have. There are Christians in the city, too, and churches, and youth groups. I will make my way in the city. It won't be Gram's way, but it will be a good way. It will be God's way.*

When Your World Is Falling Apart

"This is it. This is our senior year. We have to do it right."

Jay Wheeler had heard his friend Lewis say those words eight months ago. He remembered answering, "For sure," but what he really thought was, *How can I do it right, how can I have a good senior year when my world is falling apart?*

Jay's life had been normal up until October of his senior year—at least it had seemed normal. His parents acted like ordinary parents and like reasonably happy married people. His older sister Becky had been just like anybody else's sister—then suddenly the announcement: she was pregnant.

At least she was out of high school. But she did live at home and Jay knew that sooner or later Lewis and his other friends would find out.

His parents had found out. Boy had they ever. The argument began in October and lasted until just before Christmas. Then, as if there had been a holiday cease-fire, they started again after New Years. Sparks were flying everywhere. In several arguments they were even throwing the word *divorce* back and forth.

His parents were angry at Jay much of the time too, and *he* hadn't gotten pregnant. He had never been that way with a girl, ever. Why had Becky done it? What was wrong with her?

He knew it was selfish to think this way, but as spring came, he was afraid his sister's mistake would ruin his graduation. As he stood in front of his locker, he spotted his Bible on the shelf. What would the Bible say about his collapsing world? How would the Bible tell him to act toward his sister?

Jay didn't even have to pull the Bible out and page through it. Fragments of memory verses were flashing into his mind.

The verse fragments came through loud and clear: "Judge not." "Even if your brother [or sister] sins against you seventy times seven times, you forgive." "Don't cast the first stone."

Jay gave his locker door an exclamation-mark slam and started for home. "My sister needs me," he said right out loud. A kid leaning on the chain-link fence said, "What?"

Work and Witness

It was payday. Carla had been on her new job for one whole month. It had been a good-news, bad-news month. The good news was the paycheck and the independence. She was living in a shared apartment and her quarter of the rent, food, and other expenses still left a nice chunk to begin repaying her parents for the loans they made to get her started.

The bad news was the office staff at her job. Several of them were quite nice; they were all OK in some ways, but there was a lot of back-stabbing among the staff, and several of them, men and women alike, used foul language. And there was gossip.

Carla thought of a Bible study on James they had done in youth group during the spring of her senior year. It was Chapter 3 of James, as she remembered, that spoke of the tongue:

> The tongue is a fire.

A world of evil.

It is a restless evil, full of deadly poison.

No human being can tame the tongue.

One part of her wanted to quit the job and look for a better environment, a more Christian atmosphere in which to work. How nice it would be to work for a firm where the boss called everyone in for prayer on Monday morning, and where everyone, for the rest of the week, was helpful and sharing and forgiving and kind.

Does such a job exist? She asked herself. Was that a dream? Could a business be like a church?

Carla thought of her church. It was a good congregation and she loved it—but not everyone in her church was helpful, sharing, forgiving, and kind either. Her church was made up of sinners like herself. Forgiven sinners, improving sinners—but sinners nevertheless.

The only real difference between her colleagues at work and her fellow members at church was that at work most of them were not repentant sinners. Maybe she could do something about that. She remembered Jesus' words about being *in* the world but not *of* the world.

After she returned from banking her paycheck, Judy brewed a cup of tea, sat down, and then meditated long and hard on her job situation. She didn't want to quit, she couldn't, really. How could she get her *next* job when her resume screamed that she had lasted only a month at her *first* job.

She thought about her father. He never swore. Never. She had overheard him in conversations where the foul talk just faded away when they realized he wasn't joining in.

She thought of her mother, too, and about gossip. Her mother had kind ways of nipping off gossip before it started. She used the "20 Questions" approach. When someone would come up with a juicy tidbit of news, her mother would ask, "Where did you hear that?" When the gossiper would say, "Oh, I heard it from so and so," her mother would ask, "Do you think he's a very good source of truth?" or "Would you trust her with the story of your life?"

Slowly, Carla was formulating a plan. She felt inside that the Spirit was helping her. It was a step-by-step approach to the people she worked with. She would:

1. Keep her job, for at least a year.
2. Try hard to make them like her for who she was.
3. Use her father's method for handling the foul language.
4. Use her mother's method of dealing with office gossip.
5. Not participate at all in the petty arguing.
6. And—quietly show herself to be a Christian.

She could begin her witness in nonverbal ways. She remembered the small standing cross their church had given to her and the other seniors on Graduation Sunday. She would put that on her desk. She would take it along next Monday. Then, in small but growing ways, she would influence the office and its people. She would make a difference there. She would pray for wisdom and guidance. She—using God's power—would make it a better place in which to work.

I Studied the Wrong Stuff

Doug had just gotten back his first major test in college—in history—and had gotten a D—his first one ever. He had studied hard, too, that was the tragic part. He wasn't much consoled, either, when he asked around the class and discovered that almost everyone got C's and D's.

The problem was that he had studied the facts—names, dates, and places—but the test was on concepts. Doug had always planned on graduate school and knew he needed good grades to get in—not all A's for sure, but good grades. He decided to stop in at Professor Jacob's office and talk about his test.

"Come in, come in," Professor Jacobs said, rising from her chair. "You're in History 11B aren't you. Your name is—" she fumbled.

"Doug. Doug Davis."

"Come in Doug. What can I do for you?"

"My grade in your first test—a D. I need to do better than that."

"Did you bring your test along?" Doug pulled it out of his backpack and laid it on the desk. Professor Jacobs looked it over, read her own written comments at the end, and then said, "You studied the wrong things, didn't you?"

"I sure did," Doug said, managing a smile. "Does it show?"

"The facts show. You know plenty about when and where things happened, and who was involved. That's not all bad. But in this course and in almost all college history courses, those facts are assumed. You must go behind facts to interpretations of the past, comparisons with our own time, and even predictions of the future. Sometimes historians try to be prophets."

"You mean like in the Bible?"

"Well, not speaking for God exactly, but making educated guesses at the future based on experiences of the past. Some historians believe history repeats itself—runs in cycles."

"You mean like strict times and immoral times, prosperous times and depressions?" Doug asked.

"Just so," the professor said. They went on to talk about The Great Depression, and Doug shared some of the things his grandfather had said and experienced.

"When it comes time to choose a period for your research paper," Professor Jacobs said, "you might consider the 30s and consider using interview information from your grandfather."

Doug smiled and nodded. What a great idea. He was glad he had stopped in. Professor Jacobs seemed a lot like a friend, like an equal. Doug knew that all his professors wouldn't be that way, but he was thankful he had lucked into Professor Jacobs for history. He would study more wisely—and the term paper, that could be really something. Doug decided to call his grandpa right after supper. *Get him thinking about it,* Doug said to himself.

A Cure for Lying

Janet came home two hours late. Her parents and her friends' parents had made a sort of pact together and agreed on a time for her group to come home from their graduation party. She was two hours late.

As she stood at the door, rehearsing her story about trouble with Tim's car, Janet knew her mother would be only half asleep, the other half of her mind alert and listening for the creak of the 80-year-old steps in their big stucco house.

Should I say fuel pump or carburetor? she asked herself. She hardly knew one car part from another, but the story had to sound believable. Strange, she thought, she and Tim weren't sweethearts. They dated only occasionally. Why would anyone suspect anything? Especially her mother. They had talked; she and Tim had just talked. He had kissed her good night, to be sure, but it was just a shade more mellow than a brother's kiss. They had just talked—about graduation, about their futures, about their hopes and dreams. It was the best and most honest talk she and Tim had ever had.

Why couldn't she be that honest with her mother? Why didn't her mother trust her?

Janet thought about trust. Maybe another side of the real truth was the *she* didn't trust her mother. Couldn't her mother handle the truth? Some truths you can't hide. Like when they publish a list of traffic violators in the weekly newspaper, and there your name is, in bold print: JANET JAMESON, STOP SIGN VIOLATION, $25.

Janet had never had a ticket, but her mom always read that column. "Isn't Bob Andrews in your class?" she would ask. "He got a ticket for careless driving."

Bob Andrews' parents had to handle that truth. When Mary Jo got pregnant last year her parents had to handle plenty. *Can't mom handle Tim and me having a long— and serious—talk in his car after a graduation party?* she thought.

Janet's awareness blossomed into a new truth: Her mom *could* handle it. Maybe she always could. *I'm going to tell the truth,* she said to herself.

She creaked quickly up the stairs and in alongside her mother's bed. She bent over, kissed her cheek, and before her mom could ask, "What time is it," Janet said, "Tim and I had the most wonderful talk tonight and I want to tell you all about it."

Janet did want to tell her mom. For the first time she really did. She tried, too, until her mom dozed off 20 minutes later. Janet kissed her mom's cheek again, said goodnight, and went off to bed with the beginnings of some new feelings about mothers and daughters and truth.

How Can You Work for a Crook?

If Neal hadn't worked in Rusty Williams' bicycle shop, he never would have known. People who bought bicycles and backpacks and skis at Rusty's Bike and Trail didn't know. The people at the church, where Rusty and his family attended *regularly* didn't know. Neal figured that Mrs. Williams didn't know, either, sweet woman that she was. For sure the Internal Revenue Service didn't know. Rusty Williams was a crook. In the two years he had worked there, that truth had surfaced for Neal in a dozen different ways.

To begin with, no one knew that Neal even worked there. He didn't think much about that when he first started in his junior year. He just did minor repairs and tune-ups on bikes and was paid the hourly wage they had agreed on. It was enough. Neal loved the work and the neat people who came and went in a bicycle shop. He didn't feel underpaid.

Later on, though, he wondered why he was always paid in cash and not by check. He asked his older brother one day.

"How much is he paying you?" his brother asked. When Neal mentioned the hourly rate, his brother said, "That's 85 cents below minimum wage. You're working against the law."

"That's why he's paying me in cash," Neal said.

"Sure. No records. He doesn't have to pay insurance or workmen's compensation or withholding either. He's saving a bundle on you."

From then on Neal began to watch how Rusty conducted his business. He handled most of the parts sales in the back room, especially small parts and all used parts, on a strictly cash basis. A kid would buy a used set of handlebars for four dollars. Rusty would make a dollar change out of his overstuffed billfold, then slip the five spot back in. Likewise with a frame or a sprocket or a wheel. One day Neal kept track and counted over $85 in cash sales in the back room. No records, no state tax, no income tax.

And there were strange transactions on the cash register too. Often, when Neal would come up with a worksheet on a bicycle repair, Rusty would say, "We might as well ring that up as assembly." That was charged against new bike sales and increased his overhead on high profit items.

What got Neal was how pious Rusty always seemed in church. His head was always bowed and his hands folded. A stranger would have thought he was some sort of saint. Neal figured many people in church *did* think Rusty was religious. Many of them were customers. Neal recognized them. He wondered how many of his church's *really* religious people would buy from Rusty if they knew what a phony and what a crook he was.

Spring came. His senior year. Time was running out and Neal would soon be off to his summer job at church camp and then to college. There were days when he wanted to blow the whistle on Rusty—but who would listen and who would care and what proof did he have after all? He didn't even work there, not really. He was just an 18-year-old kid who liked to hang around in the back room and mess with bikes—that's what Rusty would say if it came to a showdown. He could make it stick, too. After all, it was his store. There was not a shred of evidence that Neal had ever worked there. If he said anything, Neal would just embarrass his parents and himself and raise a big stink—and in the end Rusty would keep on doing business as usual. Crooked.

Finally, Neal just quit. He could have worked another month, but he quit. Sure, he loved bikes, and sure, he loved Rusty's back room with the workbench and the alignment fork and the tools hung neatly on pegboard. He loved the customers too. But he just quit. He wouldn't work for a crooked, bold-faced hypocrite any longer.

Maybe the IRS would never catch Rusty, and maybe his wife would never find out, and maybe their church would never know—but one thing Neal knew for sure. God knew. God knew Rusty Williams was a crook. God knew Rusty Williams was a hypocrite. Neal knew it too. He also knew that he didn't want to be that way. Neal had learned a lot from Rusty.

Last Date

Carrie stood in front of the mirror, fussing with her hair. Tonight she would go to the Senior Farewell Party with Ron. For them it really would be farewell. She thought—no, she knew—it would be their last date.

A last date with Ron wasn't going to be easy. They had been going together (going steady, her mother would call it) for two years. They had spent so much time together in so many places. They were always together on band trips, they went together to almost every school function, and most weekends they did something together—a movie, swimming in summer, sliding down courthouse hill on cafeteria trays in winter. Sunday nights it was youth group. They were together during the meetings and afterwards, too.

Ron had been so special for so long that for many months running during their junior year Carrie thought of herself as married to Ron. Not sexually, of course, although they did get pretty physical sometimes, but more like comfortably together.

Carrie supposed that some kids—even some she knew—would do wild things on their last date of their last party of their last year in high school—a kind of last fling. Carrie wouldn't do that. But she did want to say the right things and at least make their break from each other as friends. How could she do that?

Just then her mother came in. "Don't you look beautiful," she said.

"Do you really think so?"

"Ron will swoon."

"That's just what I don't want him to do. I think this will be our last date and I don't know exactly how to handle that."

"Ron is a very special young man. Are you sure?"

"I'm sure. I think he knows, too. Lately we've been talking about the future and discovering we don't agree on a lot of things."

"Like what things?"

"Like what's important. What kind of work is important and where to live and how to spend holidays—things like that."

"Those are important, to be sure, but they're not impossible to overcome."

"I know that. But the spark is gone. Do you know about spark?"

"Your dad and I still have a few sparks left after 22 years. Yes, I know about spark." Her mother smiled as she said that and got a faraway look in her eye. Carrie wished she could see what her mom was seeing just then. She wished she had a video of her mom and dad when they were younger and looking forward to the 22 years and the four kids and the mortgage and the jobs and the zig-zag moves across the country.

Just then the doorbell rang. "That will be Ron," her mother said.

"I know. I'm half afraid to go."

"Just tell him how you feel. Tell him he's been your best friend for two years and how important that was to both of you. But your pathways are taking different forks now. All good things end—sometime."

Carrie took one more look in the mirror. All good things end. Even her parents' marriage would end someday. One of them would die and leave the other alone. *We enjoy things as long as God lets us have them, I guess,* Carrie thought.

The bell rang again, two long, insistent rings. "I have to go," Carrie said.

"Good-bye. Don't worry. It won't be so bad. God bless you my dear daughter."

Carrie went with that blessing ringing in her ears. *I guess I'm not alone in this,* Carrie thought. *God will help me—and maybe Ron will too.* She grabbed for her purse and ran for the front door.

Last Date, Part 2

Ron stood in front of the mirror, buttoning his shirt. Tonight he would go to the Senior Farewell Party with Carrie. The party was aptly named. Ron was sure that tonight he and Carrie would say good-bye after two years.

Ron thought back to their first date, a movie. He could still remember the title and much of the plot. He could also remember how nervous he was and how, afterward, as they ran part way home, he took her hand and pulled her along and how, after they were back to walking, he still held her hand—and she held his. He remembered how thrilled he was just to hold her hand.

They had long since gone past the hand-holding stage, but not way past. Ron could only imagine what it would be like to be what his health book called "sexually active," but he had decided not only that there were too many problems and dangers in that, but also that it was wrong. They had discussed these things in youth group at church and on this he and Carrie had long ago agreed. Just so far was far enough for both of them.

Some of the guys he knew would use this last date as an "anything goes" night. Not Ron. A principle is a principle, first date or last date.

Ron thought it strange that they were in such perfect agreement on sexual matters, but had lately disagreed about so many other things. Ron talked to his dad about that:

"So you and Carrie are arguing about lots of things lately?" his dad said.

"Not always arguing, but disagreeing."

"High school years, and the few years just beyond are very formative," his father said. "People change. People who hated poetry in junior high begin writing it. A kid who loathed sports in high school goes out for rugby in college—and loves it. That's why early marriages are so risky."

"Because people change, you mean."

"Sure. At 16 they think they were made for each other—then a couple of years later the person they married seems like a stranger."

"The songs are baloney then, about 'Love keeping us together' and 'All you need is love,'" Ron chuckled.

"That's for sure. Better to wait a while and marry an old friend."

"You mean like 50 or 60?" They both laughed.

Ron remembered this conversation as he said good-bye to his parents and walked out to his car. He and Carrie were friends, more than friends, but he didn't feel the same. She didn't either. He could tell. The hopes and dreams were gone, too. There was no future for them. It was all because their values were changing—or rather that they were old enough now to begin to know their own values and to talk about them.

Ron knew now that he would not marry Carrie. He knew this would be their last date. He wanted it to be a special night, though, a capstone on a long relationship that had been good for them both. Should they talk about these things right away, before they even got to the party, Ron wondered, or later, at midnight?

Ron rang the doorbell—and after a long wait, rang again—two long, insistent rings. Carrie appeared at the door, looking more beautiful than she ever had before. But that changed nothing.

Ron, thinking only of graduation and the end of their school days together, said, "Well, this is it."

Carrie took it the other way. Ron could read that in her eyes. She smiled, rather sadly, and said, "I guess it is."

"We've had a great two years together," Ron said.

"We sure have."

They walked toward the car, hand in hand. They were more together and more apart than they had ever been. Ron and Carrie had helped each other grow up.

The Chosen

I've never been one of the chosen ones. In this school
I mean. There are chosen ones. Even in grade school
you could start to pick out which ones would be chosen—and for what.

For instance: Candy was destined to be our homecoming queen. It started with the way her mother always dressed her in third grade and how she learned
to feel about herself. Later on that showed in the way
she carried herself. I wonder if her father called her
"princess" and treated her like special stuff. My folks
treat me more like Cinderella: "Wash the dishes. Sweep
the floor. Clean your room."

Then there's Jake. Who else could be both captain of
the football team and president of the student body?
He has always been athletic and has always been able
to sweet-talk anybody into anything. He should spend
his life selling used cars or aluminum siding.

And Penny. The perfect valedictorian. She has been on top of our class just about forever. The only thing she didn't ace was gym class—but that doesn't count toward your average. I'll bet if it did she'd be Olympic level.

Then there's me, the unchosen. In grade school I used to get chosen after everybody else and just before Penny when we played games at recess. In junior high I never got elected to any class offices like Jake. Now, well, put it this way: If they stood me up next to Candy, I *would* look like Cinderella—without the glass slipper and Prince Charming.

Who chooses these kids to be so special? Or do they choose themselves? Nobody has ever chosen me—except maybe God.

Wow. You know, thinking about it, that's pretty special. God did choose me and God chose some of the others, too. Most of Jesus' disciples were ordinary and unchosen until he came along. They were fishermen, and tax collectors, and people like that. Average people, I think—like me. Not the best athlete, but not the worst either. Not the smartest—but not the dumbest. And some things I am quite good at—like drawing and sewing my own clothes. Maybe God has chosen me for something special. It will be fun to put my gifts to work and discover what God has in store for me. Who knows, maybe I'll change the world!

Will's Graduation Speech

Will was clapping about as hard as the rest of them. His friend Brad had just finished his speech. Brad was valedictorian. Number one. *No reason to be jealous,* Will thought. *I deserved to be number 84. Maybe I deserved worse than that.*

They should let somebody like me make a speech too, he thought. *The "average-atorian" speech. I could tell them some things about this school and this town— and some of these teachers, too.*

Will was angry. Not furious. Not the kind of angry that sends a kid out after midnight with rocks and paint to vandalize the school. But he was angry. He was graduating, to be sure, but things could have been a lot better. He began to formulate the mythical speech in his mind. He would start this way:

"Classmates, beloved teachers (looking at Mrs. Carver and Mr. Carlson), despised teachers (looking at Mr.

Adams and one or two others), administrators—some of whom are ding-a-lings too, but I'd better get on with it—parents, ladies, and gentlemen.

"I am graduating today—but just barely. I have learned enough here and elsewhere to know that my problems at this school and in this town were and are mostly my own fault. But a school and a town can help someone like me, and that's what I'm going to talk about today.

"When my mother died two years ago, I was working at Charlie's Cafe every night—and carrying a full load at school. Suddenly dad and my sister and I were doing housework and shopping and all kinds of stuff that mom used to do. Her part-time salary was gone, too, so I couldn't just quit my job.

"That's when I started chemistry and that's when I needed a tutor or some sessions with the teacher. But Mr. Adams (looking him right in the eye), you just kept writing these cute sarcastic notes on my papers and telling me I'd have to do better. I knew that. You didn't have to tell me that. What I didn't know was *how* to do better. That's what you didn't tell me. If I had been bolder I would have asked for help. If I had been bolder I probably wouldn't have needed it anyway.

"And then along came track season. Coach McDonald (looking at him, trying not to break up), you are one of my favorite people, but you failed me too. You should have told me to quit track. You knew what I was going through. You also knew I wasn't going to win any meets or break any records. And the team spirit wasn't so good that year either. I wouldn't have missed much. I couldn't have done it on my own—but if you only had advised me to quit.

"And as for you, some of my so-called friends. . . ."

At this point Will quit composing his mythical speech. The superintendent was at the podium now, making his usual speech about the importance of a good education in preparing for the world ahead.

I got a real education in the last couple of years, indeed I did, Will thought, his anger ebbing. *It wasn't like Brad's. It wasn't quite what the superintendent is standing there talking about either, but it was an education. I've learned to cope. I've learned that I can't do it all on my own—I need to ask for help sometimes and not wait for it to be offered. I've learned how to handle some deep sadness and the moods my dad gets into and the extra work and my feelings about God— especially that. Oh, how I thought God had failed me and cheated me when mom died. But I've learned better. God taught me better.*

Will looked up at the stage, his anger now gone. This was a commencement—a beginning. Will would make it that. He would ask God to help him make it that. A new beginning. *Good thing for me*, he thought, *that they don't allow "average-atorian" speeches.*

Will I Change?

After the graduation exercises everyone was wandering around on the athletic field: graduates, parents, family, friends. Pam and Karin spotted each other at exactly the same moment. They were in each other's arms instantly.

"I didn't know you were back," Pam said.

"I got back yesterday. Couldn't miss your big day." Karin was smiling broadly.

"Is your semester over already?"

"Took my last final the day before yesterday."

"Must feel good. Two years done. You going to loaf on the beach all summer?"

"No. I'm going back next week for summer school. I'm going to try to finish in three and a half years."

"What's the hurry?"

"I want to go to law school," Karin said. "I think studying my whole last semester for my entrance exams should help get me into a good law school—maybe even get me a scholarship."

Pam and Karin wandered over to talk to friends and parents. Later that evening, between her reception and the party, Pam thought about her friend Karin. She couldn't believe the change. Karin was dressed so smartly and she carried herself like someone with an important goal. She seemed so serious.

Pam remembered the fun they had had at youth group and at Bible camp. They were known as "The Kooky Two." Always doing something nutty. During Karin's senior year, Pam had begun to miss her from the moment Karin was accepted for college. They both cried at Karin's graduation—but Pam was inconsolable. Being the one left behind was harder somehow.

But now, two years later, the two of them seemed so different. Two years away from home had changed Karin so much. Pam wondered if she herself would change. She didn't want to, not at all. She wanted to stay carefree and kooky—to stay 18 the rest of her life.

Pam thought about people she knew who acted like they were 18 even though they were middle-aged or older. Like Mr. Arvin, who built himself a powered hang glider last year, and he was already 60. Or Mrs. Selmer, the widow, who was 73 or 74 and still rode a bicycle to get her groceries.

Pam wanted to be like that—or at least one side of her did. But another side of her wanted to be grown up and suave and sophisticated. She couldn't be both.

She guessed she'd have to do like Karin and get on with it and take what came. She knew she wouldn't go to law school like Karin, but she would go to school. Maybe she could be trained to teach or to become a church youth worker. Maybe she could stay young that way.

It was hard to grow up. Pam was learning that all too quickly.

Holier Than Me

Randy and his parents spent a solid year looking at colleges. He and his mother drafted a letter in inquiry early in his junior year of high school. They mailed it to 20 colleges. Then in the spring of his junior year, after looking through the mountains of materials those schools had sent, Randy and his parents visited their four final choices.

It came down to Silver Hills, one of the good state university satellite colleges, and Trinity, one of the colleges of their church. Randy's folks wanted him to choose Trinity. They didn't say it in so many words, but Randy could sense it.

He liked Trinity a lot. It had a beautiful campus and was located in a quaint, small town. But Silver Hills seemed more his style. Randy wasn't a super-churchy kid and he knew it. He wondered if all the kids at Trinity would be "Are you saved?" types, pious beyond endurance.

Randy happened to meet his pastor on the street the week after their tour. "How's the college hunt?" Pastor Wilson asked.

"We're down to two," Randy said, "Silver Hills and Trinity."

"Your folks will want you to go to Trinity, no doubt."

"I think so."

"It's a good school."

"But won't the kids all be more religious than I am?"

"Some of them will, no doubt. But you aren't irreligious, Randy. You just aren't verbal about your faith— and you aren't very groupy—youth group and Bible camp and such."

"I know. But will I fit in at Trinity?"

"I went to a school like Trinity. I found every kind of student there from the very pious to avowed agnostics."

"Agnostics?"

"Kids who weren't at all sure there even was a God."

"So you think I'd fit in?"

"Sure. You'd fit in either place, actually. It's just that at a school like Trinity the percentage of Christian students and teachers is higher. And that means that people there will probably ask more religious questions than you'll run into at some other schools."

"I guess I can handle that," Randy said.

He thanked Pastor Wilson and continued walking down Main Street. *Will mom and dad be surprised!* he thought with a smile.

Nuclear Fears

I've been talking to other seniors. Graduation seems
to bring out our fears—or at least make us talk about
them. Like, Pat is afraid of going off to college and Kim
is afraid of leaving home and Lisa is afraid of leaving
all her friends behind.

That stuff bothers me a little bit, too, but what I've
been really afraid of (and I wouldn't dare tell any of my
friends about it either) is nuclear holocaust. Like, what
good are all our plans for the future if we blow ourselves
up?

It all started, I think, when we saw that film in history
last fall. I couldn't believe the destruction. And those
poor people who were so burned and blinded and crip-
pled. What suffering. They couldn't help themselves,
much less each other.

I began to wonder what it would be like if that happened here. There wouldn't be enough doctors and hos-
pitals. There would be mass confusion—no water or

electricity, cars would be useless too, with everything torn down and blown up.

I tell you it scares me to death—or it did until I went and talked to our pastor about it. He said that war frightened him, too, but he told me he is doing something about it. He is on several volunteer committees and gives money to them—and he writes his legislators (I guess I could do that too), and he prays for peace almost every day and most Sundays in church.

"After that," he said to me, "we must leave the future in God's hands. We do our best to make things better, then leave it to God."

After that session with him I felt better. I learned from him that peace is everybody's business. Worrying about war is wasted energy, but working for peace isn't. I wonder if there are any good peace organizations for young people. I'm going to find out. And, I'm going to pray, too.

Does He Have to Dress
Like a Trucker?

Parents' Day. Mike shuddered when he heard the announcement. Here at college he was a new person, somehow disconnected from his home and family. Everyone accepted him for just what he was, or at least for what he tried to appear.

Parents' Day. He loved his mom and dad but thought they would be way out of place here. With horror he envisioned his parents standing in the caf line, both of them overweight and not too tastefully dressed—his mom in colors too bright and his dad, as always, in his boots, brass belt buckle, and shoestring necktie.

Does he always have to dress like a trucker? Mike thought to himself. *He is a trucker, I guess. But did he have to be a garbage trucker? Why did I have to grow up as the garbage man's kid!*

Mike was proud of his parents, though, in another way. Their small business had grown steadily. His parents now ran 30 franchise trucks in three counties. They had also shown foresight, long before the ecology controversies began, to buy and register as landfills several ideal acreages that would not only last for many years to come, but also be valuable commercial property when filled and landscaped.

Parents' Day came, and so did Mike's parents. His dad still looked like a trucker, but his mom somehow looked better than he had anticipated. They were wonderfully at ease during the planned activities—especially chapel—and Mike was beginning to relax. Then they went to the afternoon reception, and Mike's geology professor, Dr. Benson, and his dad got into it.

Up to that point, no one had asked what business his parents were in. Mike hoped that no one would. Dr. Benson asked his father.

"Garbage," his father said. "I'm in garbage." Just like that. *Garbage!* He didn't even hedge with sanitary landfill or hazardous waste (their growing subsidiary).

Soon Mike's father and Dr. Benson were in a complex and technical and *heated* discussion about waste disposal. They were raising their voices, disagreeing at many points. People were listening. It was the beginning of a scene.

I knew it, Mike thought. If any of his new friends had happened by just then he would have shrugged his shoulders and rolled his eyes as if to say, "Well, what could you expect from garbage collectors?"

But just then Mike heard the discussion change tone. Dr. Benson was saying that he had never really looked at it from a businessman's point of view before. He was nodding now, and his eyes were saying, "I see." Then he was mentioning an all-college panel discussion in mid-November for their ecology conference, and how good it would be to have someone there with first-hand, practical information about waste disposal.

"Could we borrow your mom and dad for a couple of days in November?" Dr. Benson asked Mike.

"I guess so. Sure," Mike said. He would look forward to that. Might be fun. His dad had always been able to hold his own in a discussion. Mike smiled inwardly at the pun that was forming in his mind: "My dad never takes any garbage from anyone—not even college professors."

What's So Bad about Following?

Joanie could hardly wait until graduation. She could hardly wait for summer and for the next fall and for her dozen close friends to scatter like thistle down. Sure, she would miss them, but she wasn't going to suffer like Rita. Not at all. Joanie, for one, was sure she'd be relieved to get out from under the pressures of her peer group.

For as far back as she could remember, Joanie had been a follower. She had always had friends; she had always been part of a group, but never, over all her school years, had she taken any leadership roles in her peer group or in school associations or on teams. She was a follower.

Thank goodness no one had ever asked her to do anything terribly wrong. Her friends were good leaders.

But she worried some about her role. She wondered if she herself could be a leader. *If ever it's going to happen,* Joanie thought, *it should start next year when I leave this school and this town and my circle of friends.*

On graduation day Joanie muddled around her room, slowly getting ready for the ceremonies. Looking in the mirror she asked herself, *What's so bad about being a follower? All of Jesus' disciples were followers. They have been our heroes for centuries. They were great followers. Members of teams are followers, too. And the president's cabinet—at least when things are working right. And research teams. The world is full of followers. It needs them.*

Joanie finished dressing and joined her parents for the ride to school. She felt a growing pride inside. She was proud of having been such a good follower for so long.

Later, when Marlene, the eternal leader, suggested that they all sleep at her place after the party, and that they get up real late and fix a big pancake brunch together, Joanie, the eternal follower, said, "Sure. Why not? Sounds like a bunch of fun."

Status

Joel had visited several colleges before he made his decision, but at last he chose the school his parents had gone to. He thought he'd like it—and his couple of weekend stays on campus with his cousin in the dorm helped reinforce those feelings.

Joel was bothered, though, by the materialistic measurements the students seemed to use to size up each other. Joel's cousin, for instance, had one of the best stereo outfits on his floor—maybe in his whole dorm. Joel looked at it—all the black and gray metal boxes stacked and wired together like the stuff in a hospital's intensive care unit. And when it was playing, tiny red and green lights popped and flashed all over the place, and little needles on the gauges danced and flicked to the intensity of the sound. Pretty impressive. Must have cost a couple thousand dollars.

Some of his cousin's friends made their marks at college with sports cars or with clothes. Others were name and place droppers and talked of the foreign travels or what senator had been over for supper.

Joel felt like a nobody. Had this become a snob school or what? His parents weren't snobs. Had the school changed in 20 years?

His parents had been so proud of his test scores and so pleased, too, with the financial aid package he had been offered. College seemed affordable with all that help. But Joel knew that his family certainly had no extra money for a car or a fancy stereo. There was no way he could play "Who's who" at college with his cousin and that bunch.

The week before his graduation, Joel thought of college and of status and of greatness. His pastor's "graduation" sermon on the Sunday before commencement fed right into his feelings. The pastor preached about James and John and their mother, Mrs. Zebedee, arguing about greatness in heaven. The pastor concluded his sermon with a vivid picture of Jesus on his knees on Holy Thursday, washing the disciples' feet.

Jesus was the greatest person ever to live on this earth, Joel thought. *If he were a college student, he wouldn't have a car or a stereo or fancy clothes. But he would be serious about his studies and he would be a good friend and he would spend his spare time listening to other people and helping them.*

I think I will try to be like that, Joel decided, nodding and clenching his teeth. *I think I'll try to experience college as much like Jesus as I can.*

Why Doesn't God Answer?

Margie was graduating. This was one of the last chances she would have to ask such a question in their Sunday youth forum. She asked, "Why doesn't God answer my prayers?"

The kids discussed her question for most of the hour. Toward the end of the period Pastor Sharon summarized and added her own opinions. "We sometimes are too narrow in what we call answers to prayer. The Bible teaches us to see God in a kind of parental role. Do you ever ask your mom or dad for things, Margie?"

"Sure. Every day."

"Do they ever say no?"

"Too often." The class laughed.

"Maybe," the pastor went on, "maybe God sometimes says no, too. And always, underline that word *always*, for our own good.

"But what about when we can't hear God, or sense that he's listening?" someone else asked.

"That's a different story. Prayer is a way of talking to God. Sometimes it seems more like we are talking to ourselves, doesn't it?" Nods of agreement all around. "Maybe we *are* sometimes. Especially our most selfish prayers. Margie, you and Ann are good friends, aren't you?"

"Best friends," Ann said. They smiled warmly at each other.

"Well then, you can communicate better with each other than with almost anyone else, right?"

"Right," Margie agreed.

"Likewise with God," Pastor Sharon said. "The better we know God, the more we can sense God there as a best friend, guiding us, helping us, and listening to our prayers. That's why we study the Bible and go to church and share God's Word with each other—like in this class."

The bell rang. The period was over. "Let's close with a round robin." They all joined hands and prayed.

Homesick

Jim went off to college and he was homesick. He learned why they call it home*sick*. He wanted to go home so much it made him sick. He felt empty inside, hollowlike. He didn't feel like eating and he didn't sleep well either—although he *was* curled up in bed quite a bit. Sometimes, when his roommate wasn't around, he cried into his pillow.

Jim called his parents the first week and asked if he could come home. His mother seemed sympathetic but his father said flat-out, *no*. Jim knew his dad was right, at least the reasonable and rational part of him knew. He knew that if he couldn't make the break now, it would be even harder next time. But no matter how unreasonable it seemed, he still wanted to go home, to *be* home.

What Jim learned later was that, although he seemed hard-nosed about it, his dad was really quite concerned.

He called their church to get the name of a pastor in Jim's new town. The very next day that young pastor appeared at the door to Jim's dorm room.

"Pastor Collins from your home town called me yesterday," he said. "He's concerned, and your mom and dad are concerned, because you are so homesick."

Jim invited him in. He thanked God silently that his roommate was at the library just then. He was embarrassed to death. Homesickness seemed like a second grader's disease—and here he was, a freshman in college, with a terminal case.

They talked a long time. The pastor gave him a card and underlined his home address. "If you get to feeling you really can't take it any more, call me or just come on over. We'll do something. I'll stop back again day after tomorrow and we'll talk."

Jim felt a bit better after the pastor left, and the following day he found himself looking forward to the pastor's next visit. He was a long way from his parents and his home, but he had a new friend and a place to go if he really needed it.

A week later Jim *did* visit the pastor's house. He was invited for Sunday brunch after church. The pastor's wife was just as friendly—and Jim was an instant hit with their two little children. Several weeks later he began to baby-sit for them. Soon the parsonage seemed like a second home. He knew it wasn't home, but for now it would do.

Jim thanked God for his family's strong church ties. The church had been Jim's lifeline when he needed it. The connections worked, and God worked through those connections. When Jim came back after Christmas holidays, he was hardly homesick at all.

How Can I Make a Difference?

Judy wasn't despairing or anything like that, but she was a bit jealous as her senior sociology class teacher asked all of them to outline their vocational goals and plans.

They seemed pretty big time, some of them. Five in her class said they wanted to be doctors, three boys and two girls. One wanted to be a lawyer, one a pastor, one girl a missionary nurse.

A lot of them had more modest plans. They would farm or work with dad as a carpenter, or go into the family business. Judy's dad ran a hardware store. She had worked there for years. No other girl in town knew what a lag bolt was, or an expansion bit, or a half-inch street ell, much less where to find it in their store. But Judy wasn't going to spend her life in a hardware store.

No way. She wanted to do something important for the world, to help the world, to make it a better place. Problem was, God hadn't told her just how to do that yet.

As she walked toward the store after school, she was still thinking of how her life could make some difference to the world. She could come up with no grand plan, no great mission. How could she help the world?

As she waited for a light to change on Main Street, Judy saw an old man lifting a small child up to the drinking fountain on Courthouse Square. "A cup of cold water," she said out loud. "That's what Jesus said, 'A cup of cold water in my name.'"

I've been thinking too big, Judy told herself. *It's the little things that count. I've been thinking brain surgeon or missionary or ambassador. Just look at my folks, for heaven's sake, how much good they do in this town—and all they do is run a hardware store.*

Judy came to a gigantic conclusion that afternoon, and it was just in time for her graduation. *It doesn't matter,* she said to herself, *where I live or what work I do. There is always water, and there will be those who need a cool drink.*

What Did I Do to Deserve This?

Mark sat in his father's leather chair sipping a cola and feeling bad in a handful of ways. He was sick and he was disgusted and he was confused. In his hand he held the mimeographed calendar for Senior Week, the best Senior Week Central High had ever planned. Mark should know, too. He was on the planning committee. Lots of great stuff: the Classic Junior-Senior Softball Game, the class barbeque at Singing Hills State Park, the parties, the parents' reception. A great week—and Mark was going to miss it all.

"Mono," he said out loud, shaking his head, "the kissing disease. And I didn't even kiss anybody. How could God let this happen to me when I worked so hard to plan it all? Did I do something wrong? Is God teaching me some kind of lesson, or what?"

Mark knew God. He knew about Jesus and grace and forgiveness, too. He didn't live in some stone-age, eye-for-an-eye, good-for-good, evil-for-evil sort of world. But when he was knocked flat on his backside for the biggest week of his young life, he began to question what he believed.

Mark did indeed miss all the fun. But he learned some things that week about people and about God. There was no way of counting how many—because he didn't think to count—but Mark was visited by dozens of his classmates during his convalescence. One afternoon the whole Senior Week committee came to see him.

And then there was Jeanie. He and Jeanie were not only classmates but neighbors. They had walked to school together almost every day for three years. Up until Senior Week they had been friends, no more, no less than that, just friends.

But during Senior Week Jeanie came every day and described in vivid detail and with great animation and emotion the previous day's Senior Week event. Mark enjoyed hearing it from the laughing, bubbling Jeanie almost as much as if he had been there himself.

The doctor let him go to his graduation. He was weak, but he went. When the ceremony ended and they all threw their mortarboard hats in the air, Mark found himself elbowing through the laughs and congratulations toward Jeanie.

If it weren't for the mono, he thought, as they reached each other and looked at each other and then hugged each other warmly, *if it weren't for the mono, I might have missed Jeanie.*

A Martyr to Maturity

The auditorium was very quiet. Lee's older sister, one of the twins, walked up on stage to get his diploma for him. She was conspicuous without cap and gown, but almost everyone in the crowd understood why. Lee's funeral had only been the day before.

Over half the class was crying, boys and girls alike. Shirley was beside herself. Lee had been popular. He'd had plenty of friends among his classmates. He had been friendly, outgoing, the very life of the party.

It was a party that had snuffed out his life. After the seniors' last exams the previous Friday, a couple dozen of the kids went down to River Park to celebrate, to talk and eat and drink. The drinking did it.

About 9:45 their pony keg ran dry and Lee and Shirley volunteered to drive back to town for more. They never made it. Shirley wasn't hurt badly in the rollover, but she was a mental shambles after crawling back to where Lee's crumpled form was lying, and after trying hysterically to shake him back to life, only to be dragged away, kicking and screaming, by motorists who had stopped to help.

The stark images of these events had turned this into the most subdued graduation in recent memory. There were no pranks; there was no fooling around, no drinking—even by the partying crowd—before the ceremony. It was almost as if Lee had become a martyr to his class's maturity.

Every graduation party had been cancelled, too. Quite a few of the kids planned to go to the church where the youth pastor had arranged for a graduation night vigil in honor of Lee. It was a poor substitute for a graduation party.

No one wanted things this way. No one would have accepted this sequence of events if there had been any choice. There was no choice. Lee was dead; they were alive. Most of them did a lot of thinking about that.

Graduating among Strangers

Jon sat half listening to the instructions about when, where, and how to line up for graduation exercises. He only half listened because he only half cared if he lined up and marched with this bunch of strangers.

Moving to a new town in October of his senior year had been the hardest thing Jon had ever done. He didn't blame his mother, either. She had to take the advancement and make the move. Jon knew enough about corporate management to know that. There was no way they could have stayed where they were, even long enough for him to finish his senior year.

So here he was, seven months later, being graduated with strangers, kids he hardly knew, kids who hadn't really taken him in or gone out of their way to make him feel welcome.

He had learned to rationalize his way around the lone-liness and the isolation. He knew he had studied harder and learned a lot more here—like, what do you do in a study hall if you haven't anyone to fool around with? You study, of course. And on weekends when no one calls? You study, of course. And on the nights of the football games and the basketball games when you don't have anyone to go with? You study, of course.

Jon hadn't looked at his transcript, but he was sure that if he had studied this hard all four years, he would have been an honor student. Certainly, though, the good record he had made in his senior year had helped on his college applications. He hadn't had any trouble being accepted in the schools he chose.

He wondered what it would have been like if he hadn't moved. He would have been happier, certainly, but maybe he wouldn't have been able to choose his college; maybe he wouldn't have become so content to be by himself, curled up with a book. There were some good things about this lonely year.

The worst thing was that he had just begun to know and like several kids in his new school. He had made the beginnings of friendships. He was slow about that. Half-made friendships aren't likely to thrive on sepa-ration.

Next year it would be starting over *again*—but this time, everyone else would start from zero with him. They would all be college freshmen, away from home, with no friends at all on campus. Then his study habits, his ability to be by himself, and his slow but steady way of developing strong friendships would pay off maybe. Maybe this year hadn't been so bad after all.

A Dorm Full of Achievers

Cindy came to college fully expecting to plow a wide furrow, the same as she had in high school. She had worked over her transcript and her letters of application so often in the past 18 months, that the person she wrote about on the applications seemed like someone else.

That someone else was pretty special. The Cindy of her application forms was a B-plus student, had played first-chair coronet in the band, had been a cheerleader for the basketball team, had played first base for the softball team, and had been homecoming queen. That was an impressive record, especially in a school of over 800 students.

Cindy had gotten into her first choice college, certainly because of that same record and the good recommendations. Her first day on campus, the day she first met Corrine, her roommate, she thought to herself,

I'll try not to lay my big story on her too heavily. I'll let her find out all this good stuff about me slowly.

So, for the first couple of weeks, Cindy didn't talk about herself and her own accomplishments much. She mostly asked questions about Corrine. It turned out Corrine was even more of a high school hero. She had been concertmistress in her high school *orchestra*, a school with 2400 students and a 65 piece orchestra, she had been runnerup Junior Miss in her state, she held tri-state records for four events in swimming, and had been in two TV commercials.

Cindy was humbled. As she met new friends up and down the hallway, they all seemed to have distinguished themselves in high school. She began to think that this college attracted nothing but high achievers. Her pride and self-confidence were dribbling away by the day. She began to wonder if she could make it here at this prestige school.

One day during mid-term exams, she popped into the room to find Corrine crying at her desk.

"What's wrong," Cindy asked.

"I feel so stupid here," Corrine answered. "Everyone seems to be smarter than I am—and more popular—and prettier, too."

"How could you feel that way after all the stuff you did in high school, swimming records and beauty queen and all?"

"Nobody here knows or cares about what we did in high school, least of all the professors. We have to make it happen all over again here."

"I'm surprised you feel like that. I thought I was the only one."

"You too?"

"Me too."

"Do you suppose," Corrine asked, "there are lots of us? Who are insecure, I mean?"

"Maybe so. We could ask around. Maybe we should start a club or something: the *Freshman Scared-We-Won't-Make-It-Club.*"

"Might be good for laughs. Think so, 'First-chair'?"

"Maybe so, 'Runnerup'."

Prayers

Thanks for Understanding

Lord Jesus, thank you for being with me for these past few years. Sometimes it seemed like you were the only one in the whole world who understood me or knew why I was acting so strange and thinking so crazy.

Be with me now as I leave this school and begin life on my own. I don't know what's out there for me, but I guess you do. You got me through before; I know you'll get me through from here on. Amen.

Fear of College

Lord Jesus, every day that goes by gets me closer to September and to my first week at college. I don't *have* to tell *you* I'm terrified, and I don't *dare* tell anyone else. Will the competition be too tough for me? Will I get so homesick I won't want to stay? Will there be temptations too strong for me to handle? Will I be lonely? Will I make friends? Help me, O Lord!

I'm glad you're going with me, Lord. Your Book will be in my hand and your love in my heart. I don't think it will be easy, but I know that without you it would be ten times worse. Amen.

Leaving Friends Behind

Lord Jesus, I'm having some trouble leaving my friends behind. We have said we will write and call, but even so, it won't be the same.

Help me to believe that I won't really be lonely and that my friends will be OK where they are and that I will make new friends in time and so will they. Be with my mind and my heart in times of loneliness—and be with my friends in their lonely times too. Please steer a few good new friends my way—and when they come by, help me to recognize them. And thank you, Lord, for being my friend. Amen.

How Can I Thank My Family?

Lord Jesus, we've really been through a lot this past year. You've been great and so has my family. I don't have much trouble talking to *you*—I do it almost every day—but sometimes saying thanks to members of my family sticks in my throat and when the words come out, they sound awkward or hollow. Why is that?

Help me to show my thanks in other ways. Make me more helpful around the house, especially when I'm tired and grouchy. And make me more understanding of my family's moods. Help me to let them know in a thousand ways that I love them and that even if I could choose from all the other families in the world, I would still choose my own. Amen.

Guide Me to a Future

Lord Jesus, I'm lost. Here I am finishing high school and I can't see ten feet beyond that. I wish I knew something about my future. I wish you'd tell me, or show me. I haven't got a clue. What do I do next? Where do I go? Job? Military service? More school? Please help me see the way! Amen.

Help Me Handle Independence

Lord Jesus, you know how badly I have wanted to be on my own. You know how often I have gone against my parents and my teachers or have fussed and stewed when they, and everybody else, tried to run my life.

Well, now I get my chance, and do you know, Lord, I'm scared. Leaving home and making my own decisions used to sound so wonderful; now I wonder if I can handle it.

Help me handle it. Help me make my own decisions well, and when I can't make good decisions by myself, help me to recognize that truth. Then knock down my stupid pride and teach me to ask for advice. Amen.

Help Me Change

Lord Jesus, no one in the whole world knows how many stupid mistakes I've made this past year—no one but you, that is. I seem to have done one idiotic thing after the other. If all my mistakes were in the newspaper, I wouldn't have a friend left in the world—except for you.

You know my outside life is in for a big change soon, leaving home and all. I'd like you to help me make changes in my inside life, too. Help me to leave the wrong stuff behind and to make a new start in my new place. Teach me to ask you for advice before every single decision I have to make—and Lord, send me some good new friends who will lead me in better paths. Thanks a lot. Amen.

I Feel Like Crying

Lord Jesus, I don't think anyone else but you would understand how I feel, but I'm so happy I feel like crying. What a good year this has been. The music and the sports have been super—even the classes most of the time. You have put me in a terrific town and a terrific school and a terrific family and I can't thank you enough. I'm just bursting with happiness.

But it's all going to change—that's what makes me feel like crying and that's what scares me too. It's over, this part of my life. Will I ever be this happy again? Is life going to get serious and threatening and risky? Will I be worried most of the time—and scared?

I guess there's nothing to do but trust you. You've taken good care of me up until now. There's no reason to think you'd suddenly change that, is there? Well, is there? I don't think so. Thank you, Lord, for always being there—and for being so everlastingly predictable. Amen.

I Confess

I confess to you, Lord Jesus, that I have done many wrong things during my high school years. I have gossiped and lied and been suspicious and unfriendly and lots more. You know it all. I ask your forgiveness. I pray, too, that you would not only forgive me, but make my graduation a time for putting some of that stuff behind, a time of starting anew, a time for growing up.

Thanks for all the good influences in my life: my home, my church, some of my teachers. Tune me in to listen more and more to the voices that call me to a better and more faithful life. Amen.

Help Me in My New Job

Lord Jesus, as I start my new job, my new work, help me adjust. Help me to get along with my boss and my co-workers; help me to see the value in what we're doing and especially the value in my part of it. Make me a happy, contented, peace-making, forgiving worker. Help me to love my work. Amen.

A Table Prayer for Graduation Day

Lord Jesus, on such a special day as this, I'd like to thank you for the ordinary things—the food we eat day by day, the air we breathe, this home, this family. They are far from ordinary—my blessings, especially my family. They are all very special to me today, and I thank you for them and for this meal and for your love and care and for theirs. Amen.

A Prayer before Commencement

Lord Jesus, this is a big day in my life and you have protected and guided me and gotten me here. Make it a great day, Lord. Help me enjoy the ceremony, make the speaker interesting, and don't let anyone, especially me, do anything dumb or embarrassing. Be with all of us kids today, tonight—especially tonight—and throughout our lives. Make me proud of my school and my town and my family and my high school friends in the years to come. Amen.

A Prayer for a Commencement Reception

Lord Jesus, thank you for getting me through this important time in my life. Thank you for family and friends and teachers, many of them here right now, who have been so helpful to me. Make me worthy of your blessings and of their investment and their trust. Bless us all as we continue to do your work in this world. Amen.